LATCHES (THIS IS NO POET)

NEESHANT SRIVASTAVA

Made with ❤ on the Notion Press Platform
www.notionpress.com

To the one that died for me.

Contents

1. CUT TO THE LOWEST

The Mahatma, Father of the Nation,

John F. Kennedy, the architect,

John Lennon the peace maker,

And the warm bullet ran through their bodies,

That thing is up again,

It felt nice for a while,

Why my Lord,

There is no answer,

Come, please drop off, it's done, it's over,

Good while it lasted, how strange,

Why do we all hear the panic bells,

Why are we shrouded in dirt,

Why do we get the feeling, O! Lord,

Like the world would fall any moment,

Why are we so fragile,

Let peace prevail.

2. O! CHILDREN

Children of the world,
So new to the plan of resurrection,
Like the Master and the apprentice,
We all know for we have been there,
Pardon us for the road is too long,
And there shall be twists and turns,
Of a mind ravaged and caving in,
To the darkness and the evil around you,
If you shall consider but do not give in,
Like dancing shadows of lights, like hews,
We know that you will make it in the end,
You ride in the ever-changing wave,
Of the sea that's choppy or uneven,
Its waves shall give you a clue that is fading fast,
Its not what it appeared to be yesterday,
And tomorrow is a new day,
While you start the game from the scratch,
And follow the trails that lead you to far and wide,
Do not give in to the crowd of failed purpose,
That dissipated too soon,
Please hold yourself,
For there's something to see,
And we cannot tell you,
How beautiful life can be,
O! children its your day in the sun,

Take time off and do anything you like,
Like a quiet corner all by yourself,
Come home soon and dissolve,
Have faith for the evolution takes time,
It's throwing hints at you,
Please be calm,
The finishing point is not far away,
Then you shall have a name in this world,
Your own name,
Your own style,
O! children tears are not enough,
For the journey is very long and hard,
A tribute to the person that you are,
That fights till that day of glory,
And never gives in,
Hang on for He has heard you,
And He is coming to join you
O! children,
You are the sweetest thing on earth,
And we are all with you.

3. LONG WAY HOME

We are all silent strangers,
Sitting with our faces turned,
Like my father said, 'cobwebs galore',
A wise friend said,
You must know when to say something,
And when not to say something,
We are all diminished idols,
Our faces have blurred with time,
I don't know this man anymore,
When it just takes a subtle gesture,
To know what that man is all about,
For we are all the same,
And yet we have sown seeds of black,
And it's hindering us to get anywhere,
Brothers are not brothers anymore,
And the silly temperature of the morning tea,
Is enough for a tiff and a bigger quarrel,
And off we go to the lady with a blindfold,
And she doesn't see anything,
For there is nothing at all to see, my friend,
We are sitting alone far away,
Hoping that someone could hear our cries,
Someone would know that the pain is real,
And it's been raging on for too long,
I must now take refuge in God's eyes,

For I must ask for justice,

There is no point when we are all too old,

And finally realize that it was nothing but a filled-up balloon,

What happened to our youth,

It was always burning and burning,

Keeping us away from our dear ones,

When something inside us just died,

And squared our view for jitters,

Rise O! man of just,

There is someone that loves you,

And you are incomplete without them,

One glimpse, two eyes are good enough,

Rest is darkness that was never a good thing,

It's a long way home.

4. A GIFT

I am planning a gift,
I don't need to look much,
I am blind and there's a cloud I see,
It's hanging low like a black smoke,
I am searching my family,
No one leaves a clue anywhere,
Mother is too high,
The cloud says it's been hanging for ages,
I don't see at all,
Someone pushes me through the clouds,
And like daylight clarity,
I cannot believe my eyes,
I am trying to catch up with myself,
Clear skies and it's blinding,
I certainly don't belong to this space,
I have walked through the same lanes for eternity,
It trips and falls,
Like I am being booked at every corner,
Like my eyes are hiding something,
When they are not,
People call it 'clouds',
I call it nothing,
This time my eyes are stone,
Like Al Pacino in one of his classics,
Like John Lennon is his round glasses,

People call it a catch,

But my eyes have evaporated,

Or is it me that has evaporated,

I don't feel a thing,

I don't hear anything,

The falling lends a warning,

Look down, you moron,

Hide behind your eyes,

And still people call it a catch,

I feel happy inside,

I cannot explain,

Words in my mouth have flown,

And new words sunken too low for me to utter,

My words are of etiquette and respect and love,

I have become the ground, the roots,

That speak not harshly ever,

Sometimes I feel I am faking it,

But I am not,

Truth is a strange thing,

Too strange for the limits that we are,

Poverty is too deep in me,

In the purest sense,

It has taken a final seat,

It's the crack of humility, great humility,

And I don't remember how poor I have been,

For I belong to an upper middle-class family,

That started with just above middle class,

Where there is no dearth of money to speak of,

Where a college is followed by marriage and then a good job,

And a lot of money,

And a lot of misunderstandings,

That's the usual pattern of life in our community,

I am poor but I am rich,

I don't know why I followed that trail,

For I am the most foolish man you'll ever meet,

And don't expect me to solve complexities,

I just give a phone call,

And ask the expert to do the rest,

I cannot say how and why I am the earth,

I have lost everything except the soul,

That's hanging around for good reasons,

I don't know how I got here,

They are listening and I don't understand why,

My mind is churning out something good,

I am fixated to human suffering,

I can even feel the pain, almost,

The gift is for someone that I met twenty-one years ago,

Life is a flicker, it will vanish before you see it,

And we are oriented to the noise,

I take that road pretty casually,

I walk but I don't know where I am headed,

I am dead for the world and have been that way forever,

Like a junk that has gathered a thick layer of dust,

It's awful to look at and means nothing at all,

I am the psychosis,

It's got no head or tail,

Like parallel rail tracks that never end or meet,

I am the 'noun' that each one of us must have,

And a very sickening 'noun',

Like a grave disease and a disability,

Like invalid,

Suddenly out of nowhere,

I am being hounded,

Like my engine has suddenly started,

Afte lying idle for a lifetime,

When there was no 'hope',

Everybody struck me off,

Like I was nothing more than soil,

Even lesser than,

And suddenly I have dreams,

I have a profession,

And they are happy to have me,

Something tells me that a woman is on her way,

Fifty years,

And God is the kindest I have ever known,

And with such a big heart,

I am poised on the gift, please,

I am looking ahead,

What is twenty-one years,

Nothing at all.

5. BECOME ASHES

Torn people of ages,

Hope is the breath that still echoes,

In the walls of old,

Saying don't let go,

Someone cried, become ashes,

If you can carry the mantle,

Never easy, you shall be sold for chips,

One slight and it's all over,

There is this persisting rhythm,

It's trying to seep into you through the kink,

Become ashes, my son,

And you shall feel the freedom,

You shall then never be sad,

For there are odd shapes and sizes around,

And the one that comes right through your home,

She carries a gun somewhere,

She is the smiling assassin,

She's prodding and prodding for ages,

Like you have no one to fall to,

Son, don't despair, be strong,

Wait for God's call,

Do what you must, but don't give in,

People have the sage and then the inner devil,

She is just a disturbance,

Jut breathe her out,

And I know you can,

For you are already free,

And there is nothing to worry at all.

6. QUIET MARTYR

I did not see,

And I am living a life,

Twenty-one years, and it's ringing too loud,

My brother and his twisted sinews,

His life in shambles,

He's poked by the young, he says,

He's a middle-aged man now of fifty-one,

Our bodies are disfigured by time,

For our own good,

There's no one at the door, finally,

And I feel I don't know anything about anything,

Like the lowest human that ever can be,

I don't know what to do,

The quiet martyr has slain me through the heart,

I feel like drowning in the river, for heaven's sake,

I know not what each human has to go through,

The list is growing and endless,

They have finally found peace,

And so have I,

Life has just begun, albeit a tad late,

I think I will thank God,

He's been very kind,

He has such a big heart,

And I am still with great happiness within,

I think I will explode,

I have so much to do,

I am so excited,

Does anyone know,

Twenty-one years, ladies and gentleman,

And the couple still survives, together,

I am just a little boy,

And I see hope all around,

I am a middle-aged man of forty-nine,

I salute the people that laid down their lives,

All for the happiness of those eyes.

7. (just) A KNOCK

I suffer for I am young,

There are eyes dropping on me from everywhere,

I need those eyes for I cannot take it anymore,

Someone round the corner is chasing me,

I don't know what's so inviting in me,

They are pouring in words I never heard before,

I fly away far into another country,

For reasons I cannot hide,

I have fallen to the lowest O! Momma,

I need to hide away from you,

I raise the greatest gamble of my life,

Someone in a ring of a finger invites me,

And I like a boy to touch I take a huge risk,

He leads me to a hotel of clients,

I am the most shameless face on the earth,

I am about to kill myself,

Like I had known it from before,

He says they do it for the money,

He bids me goodbye and walks off,

Its five in the morning and I hear a knock,

I am asleep but partly awake,

I begin to push myself out of the bed,

In a lunge to answer the call,

Just then the knock suddenly ceases,

And I find myself back to sleep,

Until I realize who was at the door,

Just two seconds away, children,

Something pushed me back to my bed, I'm sure,

I wake up,

And the kind manager points me towards the bus,

As if he knew what was going on,

I have forgotten everything about the morning,

Until late in the night I am about to embark,

On the trails of the morning person,

'Please do not step out Sir',

Manager is firm and precise,

'They'll catch you and put you behind bars,

For no reason',

I obey and I obey,

I head back home a long way,

Just two seconds like a shield and I am saved,

Youth is a very dangerous thing,

One pulse can smoke the life out of you,

I have mostly walked on a knife edge,

Each time saved and saved, I don't know why or how,

How can I explain what I have found,

After years and years of dreaded youth,

For now I have tremendous peace around me,

I am no more in the eye of plenty or anyone, maybe,

I sit in my quiet room, silent with great maturity,

I am now a pure 'human',

Forty-seven years and a relentless walk,

I am safe and sound, for all my brethren,

My eyes have a deep passion,

Like a great piercing precision,

I know people, yes, I do,

Wearing a common attire,

Those people that died for they felt they had to,

And there is no other way,

A strong army of evolved people,

Ready to take on the world,

With a calm and a quiet demeanour,

In a state of constant rest,

And complete peace.

8. WHERE IS MY FAMILY

I live in half-baked truth,

Time is running away,

I have beaten my body hard,

Pushing it to the limits and showered bad words,

I am turning my head around in great hurry,

To the watch on the wall,

It's telling me as a hard task master,

It's time to move and get on with it,

I feel I have not done enough during the day,

I feel I am missing something crucial,

My body is out of shape,

I have torn my body to pieces,

I have no mercy at all,

My body has taken me through the path,

Until I got home,

I cannot thank it enough,

Now I have given up my body, and let it go free,

It has melted the fever,

I don't feel anything around people,

I have even sought the courage,

To invite my brother and his family,

That lives not here, but far away,

A man and his wife,

I have not spoken to her for fourteen years,

And I don't live in my body anymore,

People jog their eyes with a sudden inflection,

I don't feel a thing,

I push my mind to gather,

It's showing me nothing at all,

Yet I do know what I see,

God the great Pusher,

He is out to make a mess of everything,

He enjoys the human and the emerging obscenity,

Too close for comfort in a room full of men and women,

All seated in their chairs, close,

That a decent man has to shut his eyes,

And his senses,

But I don't do nothing at all,

I say let it come, let it come,

And I do not challenge Him, never at all,

I am the one, please someone kill me,

I am, yes, I am, and I am shameless,

And I lift my head and the sound of lashes,

From sharp daggers, maybe not,

It has reduced to an imagination,

I am living in thin air,

I see and I see nothing at all,

People act strange, they do,

And I am not looking, please,

I have become used to, maybe twenty-nine years,

God's greatest gift, finally,

It's been tough, very tough,

And I am a scared baby,

Finding a corner to make funny sounds,

Like a little child and a delightful candy,

People make big, which I am certainly not,

I am just trying to make some calculations,

Setting things right, like arranging books on a shelf,

I am all alone, and I love it,

I only know that I miss my family,

I cannot believe the coldness for so long,

What took me so long,

I am running out of time,

Sixteen years could be thirty-two,

In a matter of seconds,

And why is everyone so relaxed,

Just like a boy of seven turned forty-nine,

Go find your family, before it's too late,

For lately I have realized one thing,

Love has immense power,

It can even bring together,

Your lost family right away,

I am flying too high and too fast,

Like a MIG, maybe,

And I feel that I am too slow,

And people have walls and clouds,

When there is nothing there at all,

We take too much time to realize,

Save your day by some ringing declaration,

Like going berserk, loud and its tangy, but salty,

Look around, everyone is fast asleep.

9. CAPTAIN OF MY SHIP

I am the captain of my ship,
The ship is on the shore tied,
I see someone on the high seas,
It is a ramshackle ship,
It only hears the waves and the crack,
Or a widening crevice,
It is surrounded by mountains of waves,
On scary dark nights,
It is broken, completely wrecked to the hilt,
Yet not broken or wrecked at all,
Run away, there is time to see,
A beautiful world, quiet and warm,
Do not come near,
You shall perish in seconds,
Or a sudden twist in the marrow deep,
I cannot turn away,
For God sakes, they are my own people,
They need a helping hand,
Not that they need a helping hand,
But how can I run away from,
My own blood, my own heart,
I can feel those forest woods,
That make the hull of the ship,
They are almost, yet they are not,
If they are fire, then I am the fire too,

I push the ship deep into the waters,

I push hard until the overturn and destruction,

I am deep in the waters,

My ship is none to speak of,

My people are searching for me, high and low,

Lo someone has dived in and pulled me up,

I am unconscious but not dead yet,

I travel on their ship for the rest,

They know something that I don't,

And I don't care,

I am one with my people again,

And a gush of happiness has risen from somewhere,

And I am wondering what happened,

Those people are laughing with tears,

They are watching me from somewhere,

And I just want a hot cup of tea,

For I survived,

Here's to the mighty Almighty,

I cannot believe my eyes,

Sometimes I stand scared, I am really scared,

I am not, but I can take it now,

I am still and the world is beautiful,

God knows what I did.

10. SPLEEN WEATHER

The weather wrote the day,
There is no sun out today,
It's a spleen weather,
The rubbish is out in plenty,
Loneliness is hurting,
Someone please,
It's the season of fresh games,
For the screech is deafening,
Everybody is looking around, hunting,
The weather has left them and the gloom hangs,
Nature looks like a colourless dull grey,
It's the end,
There's nowhere to go,
The poet has lost his poetry,
Someone is trying to keep warm,
The girl parks her scooty and walks,
Someone has seen her and she's game,
Eyes are thrown everywhere,
It looks like the end of the world,
I cannot go on further,
There are people and I must not go on,
Mind holds on the singular,
Like it always did,
SUV's and cars are turning and turning,
They don't know where to go,

Human race a gimmick,
It's the venting season,
Day and days without the sun,
Is sure to bring out the evil,
God is playing on the senses,
Looking in the eye of each one passing,
The young ones are the worst hit,
But young ones have already matured,
They are young no more,
I am happy today,
I have found something,
By means of a profession,
And I am not growing any younger,
God is kind, very kind,
I didn't know that there is place,
For people like me,
I think I shall make inroads now,
I have funnel fisted the Master,
He has read my spleen,
And I bow before him when I leave,
Show me something O! Master,
My eyes are too eager,
I shall conquer the weather,
And the heat of second half classes,
I shall fluff up the ambience,
And bring a smile on my Master's lips,
I shall dive in with him,
The spleen weather has turned cheerful,
I walk among the shadow of lights,

To lighten up the air post twilight,

I am so happy,

I cannot but repeat the words,

I sit in awe like always,

For the limitless beauty around me,

Until I forget my feet,

And I think it will fall on me,

But I don't think it will now,

I have become the father of the baby,

That I was.

11. MONEY IS TOO POOR

Mind sinks too deep into subtleties,

Infinite power it seems,

Working on the nonphysical,

Like surreal, too sublime,

Building something block by block,

Heading too far into an outrageous technology,

The fuel pumped in to reach an impossible dream,

Have we gone too far,

Just to please a handful of 'rich',

Who have no sense of a simple word like 'life',

The makers tiring indefinitely to bring out the inner,

Like they had seen something,

They wanted to share,

That 'black' boy and that ravaged little 'girl',

With those dreams of 'food' all day,

Man in deep thought,

Don't forget,

It is out of poverty that that mind rose,

Poverty of body and poverty of spirit,

To carry a great load that is 'unjust',

While the rest rolled and rolled on,

We serve the rich, my friend,

Money is poor, very poor,

It cannot buy you a night of peace,

That which great poverty can,
Rise and rise, it's getting harder and harder,
O! man of steel, it's time and time enough,
Don't you ever dream of heaven.

12. THERE'S A MAN

There's a man that stands,
Far away from his hilly home,
In the planes of a land of impoverished people,
That do not speak his language,
In a lost count of time,
Coloured black in the harsh sun,
With a home far away of fair skin,
He won't say a word, his eyes of marble,
He has found something he cannot describe,
Year and years and his voice proud and bold,
His sons follow him,
Followed by his grandsons,
He's got red beetle leaf stuck in his teeth,
He's in the land of Buddha,
There's something here, he cannot leave,
He has found home far away from home,
People and people and the untiring melody,
There's no one that hung around so long,
I have never seen him say,
He belongs to the hills,
He's got idols of Laxmi Ma and Ganesh Bhagwan,
He bows at them with each sale,
He's the man in this land,
He guards the place,
With the eyes of the hills,

A Hindu, A Buddhist, A Christian,

I can never forget him,

He is a kind man,

I am but a baby and he knows me,

I cannot believe I met him,

Such people dazzle the place and bring happiness,

He shall be beside me,

Till the day I die.

13. LATCHES

I heard of latches,
A good man and his limit,
God above in His latches,
Some too soon, some later,
And I am walking alone, all alone,
It's been a long time,
The tears keep coming,
They don't cease,
A pond, a lake, a river, an ocean,
Why this done to me O! Lord,
Where in the world did I gone wrong,
Are you not counting me, and why,
Where are my Latches,
O! Maker of the world,
I am weakest of the lot,
And You don't think so,
Don't Come to me and propose,
A deep and impossible challenge,
I am too possessed, don't You know, Sire,
No please, it's getting too hard for me,
I can't take it anymore,
Give me my Latches,
And send me, wherever You choose,
I'd rather be an idle ant, floating around,
Rather than worrying of building,

A mud baked house of pores,

And finally, No Latches,

Really.

14. TODAY I KNOW

Today I know,
Yesterday it was forming,
It takes a long time,
And you ought to know that,
All my friends out there,
A very Good Evening! to you all,
I salute you for you are my shining light,
With tears in my eyes,
I have landed in your land, O! Sire of ages,
I feel like a rookie,
A little child am I,
I never knew and it took a long time,
How you are knocking it off, every day,
I do get the sense, Sir,
Great shapes, I love it,
And your eyes, Sir,
All of fire,
I think I have been fooling around,
You know, yada, yada, yada…,
What have I said,
I am embarrassed, please,
But you don't care,
And you wink at me in delight,
Wow! What great company,
I have told Him, Sir, very clearly,

Stop shooting arrows, for God's sake,

I am done,

Don't test me now, stop please,

I am in the village, finally,

And am having a whale of a time,

Baby, baby, baby, who's looking at me,

Please turn your gaze, it's just a fool,

My God, are you kidding me,

Seriously, I never thought,

That life would end this way,

Where was I, never mind,

All those dark nights are over,

And I am…,

Turned into a poet, I feel,

Who cares,

I am just diving into your World, Sir,

I am gone,

Let's get together Sir,

And have a party,

And don't expect me to meet your eyes,

I am the shy one, that's right,

Ga, Ga,ga,ga,ga,ga,ga…

15. TUMBLING TODDLER

See the tumbling toddler,
Mother is nowhere to be noticed,
It has taken a fall from the fluff,
Its head is hit on the hard ground,
It's gotten a boring bump,
It can hear the honkers loud,
The smooth jazz is the jostling joint,
It has survived in a surreal swamp.